Life is beautiful

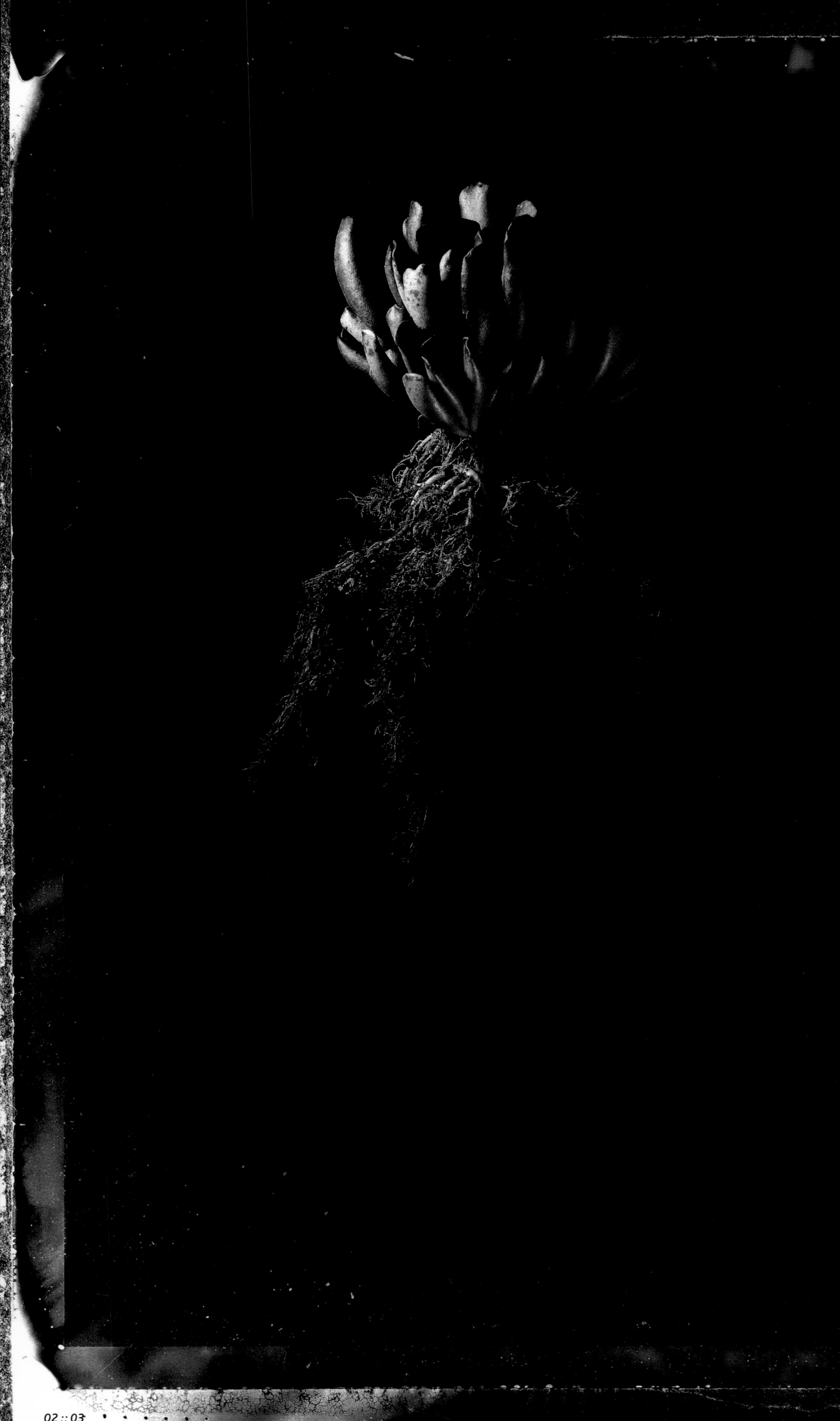

bold

honest

individual
intriguing

graphic

electric

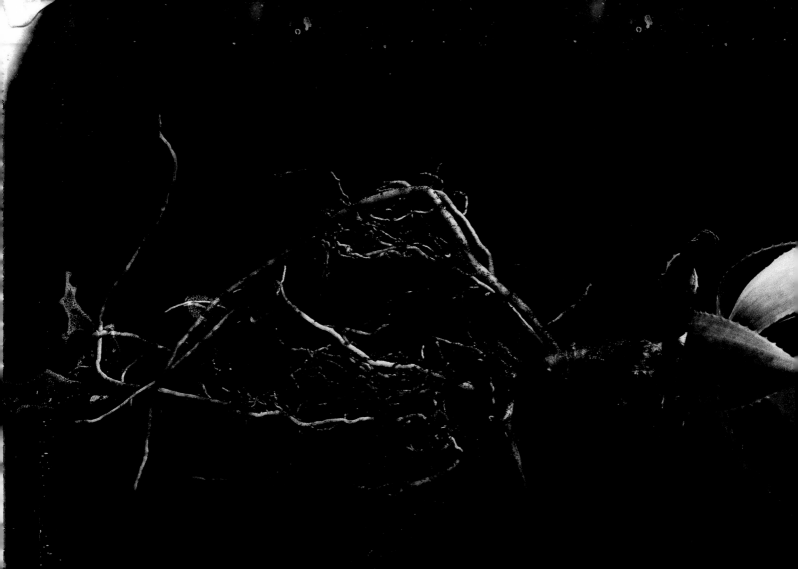

First published in August 2007

First edition

Published by Fotografik Communications in collaboration with Slipway Books, South Africa

Copyright © Fotografik Communications, 2007

www.fotografik.co.za

Photographs copyright © Clinton Friedman, 2007

Text copyright © Clinton Friedman and Siobhan Gunning, 2007

The moral right of the author has been asserted

All rights are reserved

Without limiting the rights under copyright reserved above,
no part of this publication may be reproduced, stored in or introduced into a retrieval system,
or transmitted, in any form or by any means (electronic, mechanical, photocopying, recording or otherwise),
without the prior written permission of the copyright owner and the publisher, Fotografik Communications, of this book

Printed and bound by TWP SDN BHD Malaysia

ISBN 978-0-620-39053-8

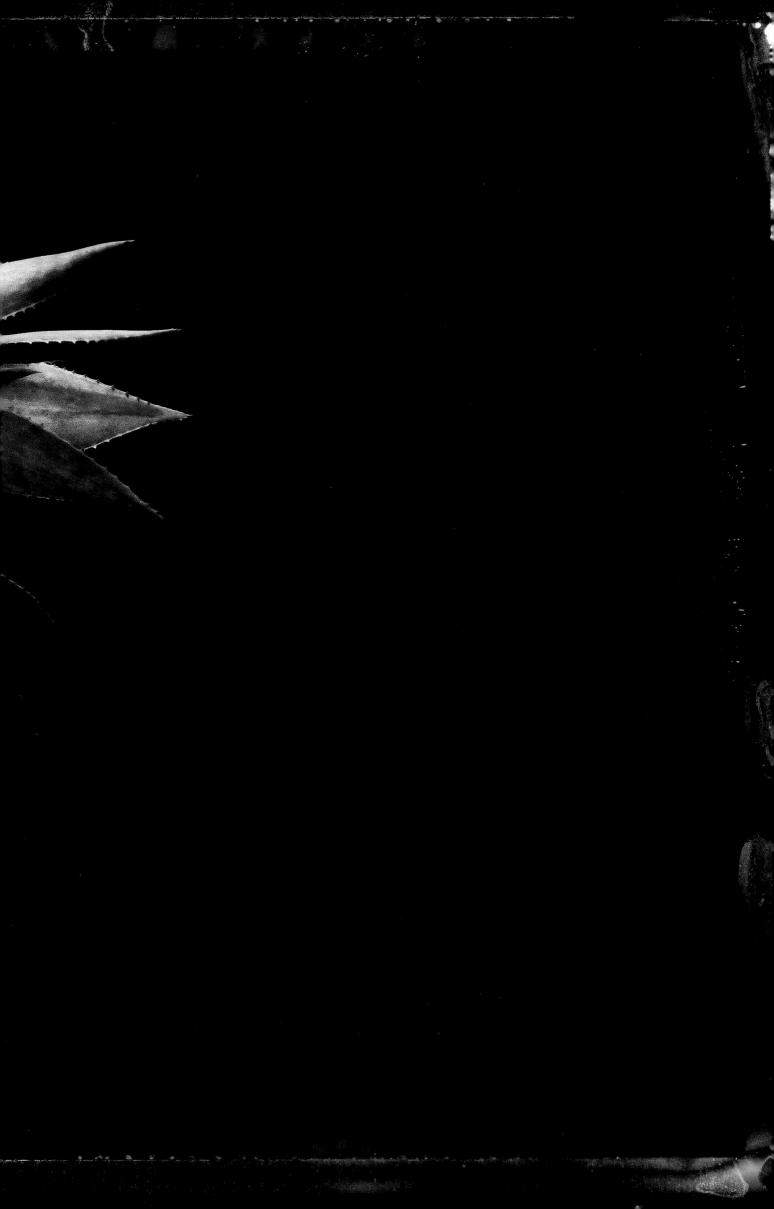

www.clintonfriedman.com

Original limited edition archival prints can be ordered online from www.clintonfriedman.com

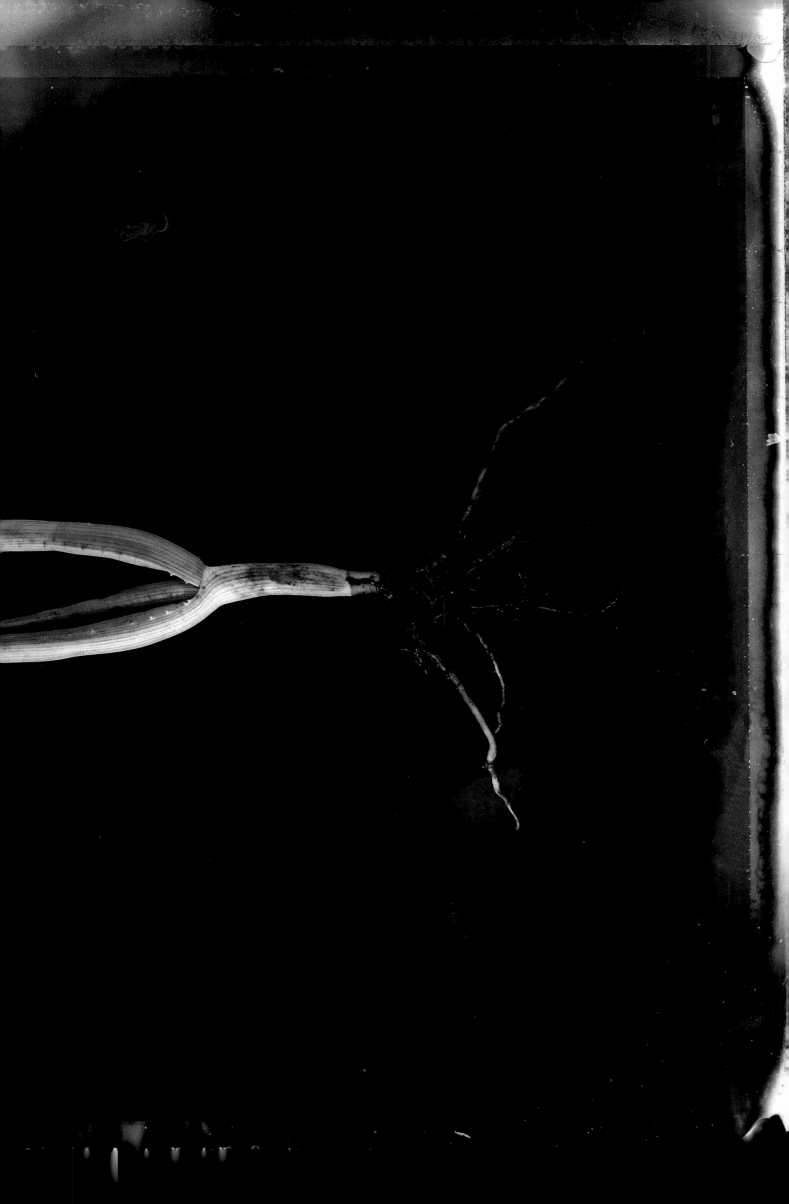

Dedicated to Bronwyn, Ethan and Ella

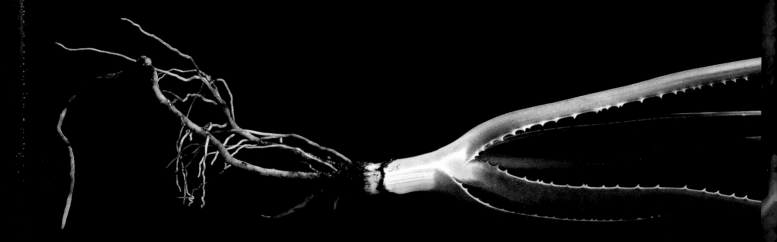

Photography	Clinton Friedman
Text	Siobhan Gunning
Art direction and design	Fotografik Communications

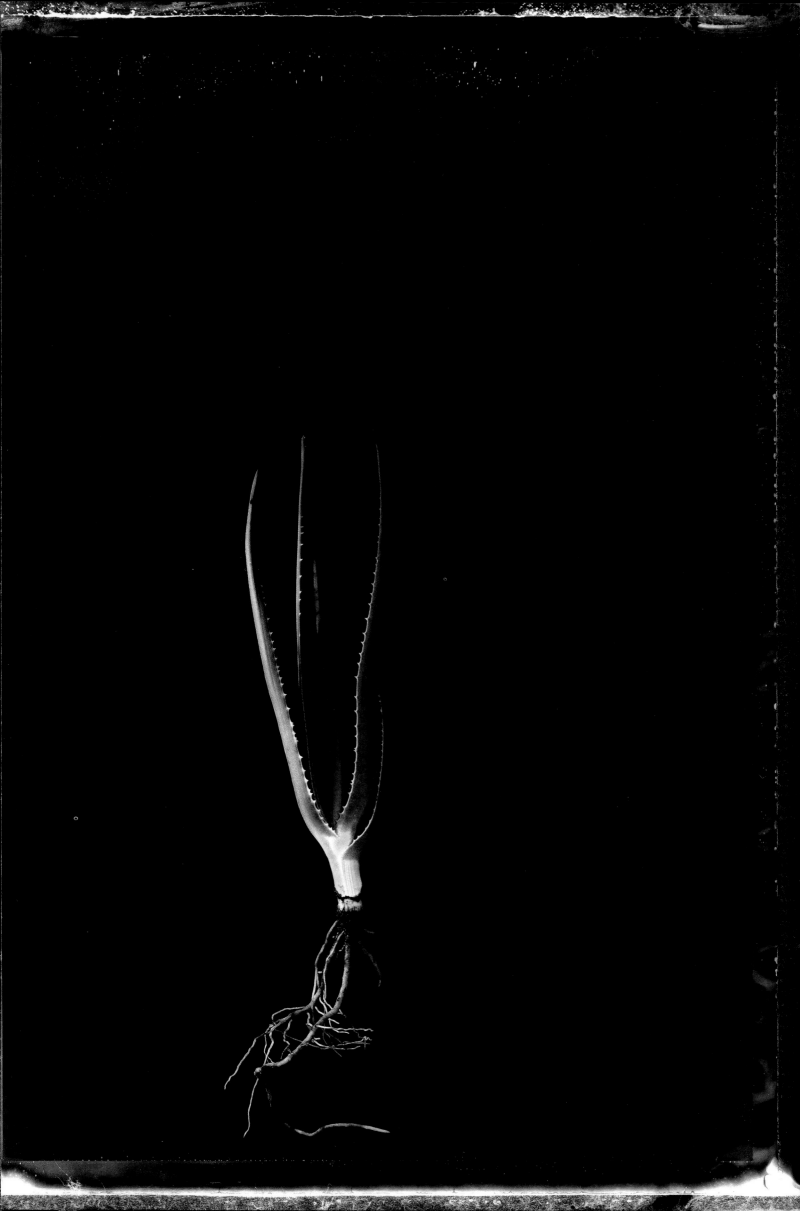

Introduction

$\mathcal{D}$isguised, faded, bruised and torn. Chopped, stacked and waiting for purpose. This is how photographer Clinton Friedman first saw the broken aloes and various herbs on his first visit to a traditional *muti* (medicine) market in KwaZulu Natal, South Africa.

These plants had been uprooted from the wild African land and transported on foot, by train and on the most precarious form of transport, the renegade African taxi (usually less than roadworthy and driven at death-defying speed). Dried, twisted, mashed or miraculously holding some of their original form, the plants are sold in a makeshift market on the pavement of the station, on the side of the road or in tiny downtown shops in areas where many fear to tread. These are healing plants, they have the power to transform, to magically reinstate the health of the sick and weary. They are blessed botanicals that have died so that others may experience heavenly health. Or that are just hanging in there, desperate for water and a fresh start in life. Which is what Clinton gave them, replanting them in his garden and then, once they were fit enough, extracting them momentarily from the ground and capturing their beauty intact on film, the giant roots of the aloes still clinging to fresh clumps of mother earth. Just as the *muti* merchants had subtracted the plants from their land in order to help other humans become whole through their return to health, so Clinton gently removed the plants just long enough to photograph and record them in their entirety, creating a historical collection for the future to remember.

Each image is a celebration of life: bold, graphic, individual, absolute and honest.

"Walking through the intoxicating buzz, my body charged by the energy around me, I select my disguised subjects. Capturing in my mind, a reflection of a youthful presence below the almost dead facade of the selected specimen. From the market each specimen travels through a rehabilitation process. This process introduces the rescued specimen back to the earth and allows them to be reborn. When back to their former glory I temporarily remove the plant and capture it on film."

Aloe dyerii

Flowers from February to June
Occurs in shady areas in river valleys
This species is not threatened
Named after Sir William T. Thiselton-Dyer

Scilla natalensis

Traditional treatment for internal tumours, boils, fractures and for lung disease in cattle
Poisonous to sheep
Used to make soap by the native people of KwaZulu Natal
Grows in damp grasslands, cliffs and rocky slopes
Bulb grows half way above ground
Leaves are hairless and velvety
Veld fires induces flowering

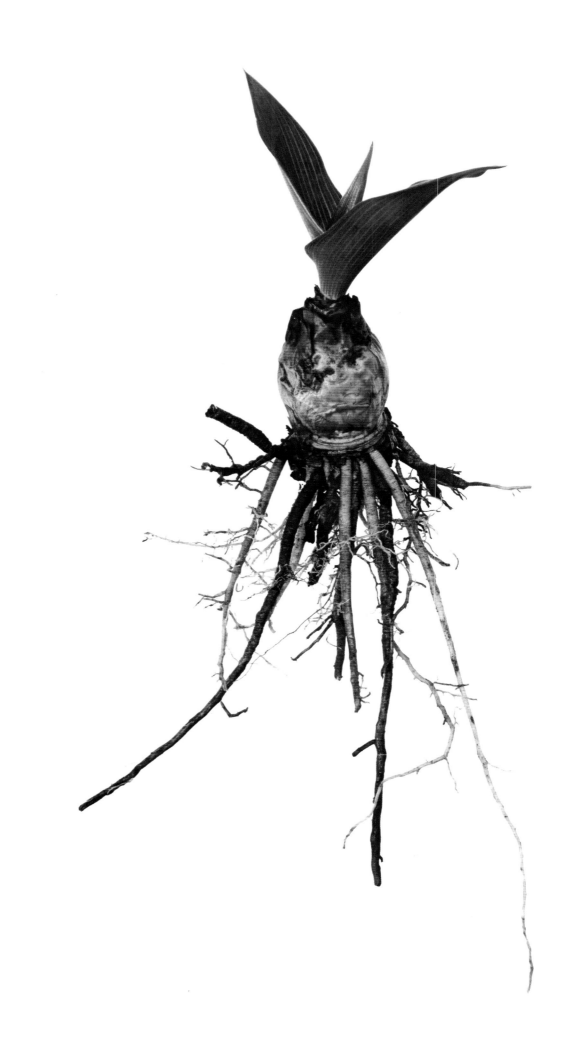

Aloe kraussi

Named after Christian Krauss, 1812-1890, German scientist, traveler and collector
Zulu name is iSiphuthumane
Grows in grassland, on sandy soil and rocky ground, up to 600mm
Young inflorescence can be eaten as a vegetable

Aloe humilis

Dwarf aloe +- 100mm tall
Flowers from August to September
Usually occurs in dense groups of up to ten or more rosettes
This species is not threatened
Aloe *humilis* is rather variable and several varieties have been recognised
Humilis means low growing

Erythrina latissima

Leaves and bark are eaten by elephant
Ash from the tree's bark is used medicinally
Sturdy small to medium sized deciduous tree
Seeds are orange to red with black spot, commonly known as the lucky bean

Crassulaceae species

Delicate soft shrub
Attracts butterflies
There are +- 300 species in the Crussula family
Crassula or crassus means thick, refers to fleshy leaves

Protea speciosa

Speciosa means handsome or good looking
Widely dispersed in the coastal mountains of the south-western and southern Cape
One of the most striking Proteas growing on Table Mountain
First observed and commented on in 1672

Erythrina lysistemon

Common name is Coral Tree
Zulu name is umSinsi
Occurs in bushveld and coastal bush
Flowers are rarely pink or white
Various parts of the plant are used for medicinal and magical purposes
Seeds contain toxic alkaloids as well as anti-bloodclotting substances

Muti

$\mathcal{W}$e are bound by our own mythology. As long as we believe, we are. And on that starless night when thunder and lightning divided the sky, we were born. It was the night Unkulunkulu, who grew out of a reed in the marsh up North called Uthlanga, grew too heavy and fell to earth. He brought forth the Zulu people and their cattle. And he created everything that is – the mountains, streams, lions, snakes, and the healing Aloe plant.

He taught the Zulus how to hunt, how to make a fire and how to grow food. And he gave certain privileged plants the power to bring any man who has lost his way into sickness back to his natural state. He called these plants *muti* (medicine). And to make sure that he had every type of illness covered, Unkulunkulu created over 3 000 species of medicinal plants. Yet he gave the ability to understand them to only a few men, the *izinyangas*, herbalists, and the *izangomas*, diviners. These wise men are the servants of the suffering and they understand that disease encompasses physical sickness together with misfortune and imbalance. They believe the spirits of our deceased ancestors, are often responsible for sending illness because the living have neglected the customs of the home and important rituals or have disrespected their elders.

To reinstate their patients' harmony with the universe, resulting in good health, the traditional healers will administer medicines that are usually of vegetable origin to treat diseases or ailments. These raw herbs are ground into powders that must be taken with water, or boiled as barks or roots that are drunk as decoctions. Other *muti* must be bathed with, rubbed into incisions, inhaled as smoke, nibbled on or licked by the patient from his fingers.

contintued on page 50 :: 51

Boophone disticha

Common name is Poison Bulb or Sore-eye Flower
Disticha means in 2 rows, refers to leaves
Used to plug sour milk containers
Bulb poisonous to live stock
Bulb used by the San people for poisoning their arrows
Used in traditional medicine to treat pain, wounds and as narcotic
Veld fires induces flowering

Bulbine natalensis

Infusions of the roots are used for diarrhoea, convulsions and diabetes
The leaves are filled with a clear gel, similar to Aloe vera gel
The fresh gel has healing properties good for burns, wounds, cuts and abrasions, due to the glycoproteins

Aloe species

Dwarf aloe +- 100mm tall
Flowers from July to September
Indigineous to mountain regions of central Africa
Grows in small clusters, rarely as an individual specimen

Aloe ferox

Flowers from May to August
One of the most widely distributed species
Occuring in a wide range of habitats, on mountain slopes and flat open areas
This species shows remarkable adaptability in terms of rainfall
Aloe *ferox* is not threatened
One of the few recognisable plant species to be found in San rock paintings

Kniphofia caulescens

Common name is Red-hot Poker
Grows in marshes or on damp mountainsides
Often grown around rural homesteads as a charm against lightning
Flowers from January to March
Zulu name is uMathunga

Strelitzia nicolai

Common name is Natal Wild Banana
Occuring in coastal dune vegetation and adjacent inland areas
Glossy green blade like leaves become split by the wind
Flowers are eaten by Vervet monkeys

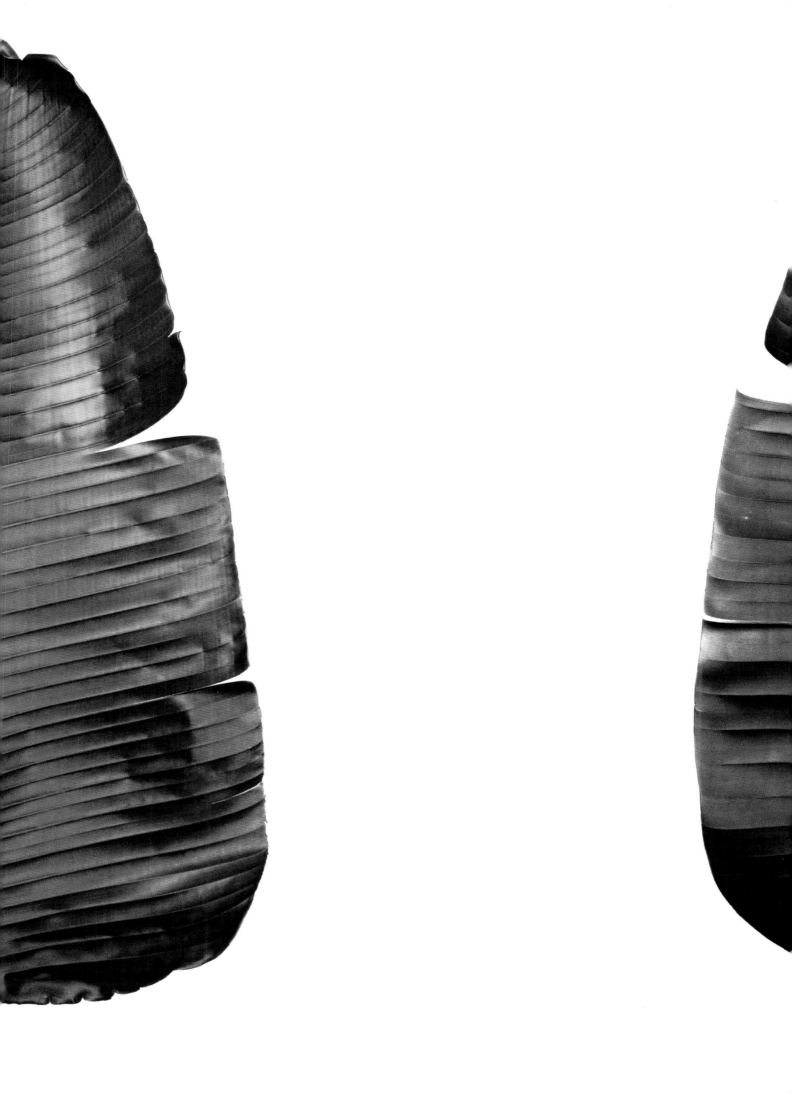

Aloe arborescens

Arborescens refers to the tree-like habit
Plants form large, many-branched shrubs or trees of about 2m high
Flowers from May to July
Flowers are rarely yellow
The species occurs from the Cape Peninsula of Southern African up the coast to Malawi
This is the third widest distribution of all the species of Aloe

Gasteria species

Flowers from June to September
Occurs in dry, remote and mountainous areas of Central Africa
Used in traditional medicine to treat hysteria and for protective charms

When Unkulunkulu created these medicinal plants, he singled out the aloe as his favourite and bestowed upon it magical healing powers. Of the many different aloes he made, he was most partial to the Aloe ferox, known also as the Cape Aloe or Bitter Aloe due to the taste of its sap. It's been used for the past 200 years as a purgative (or, as the Zulus say, "to clean the blood") and is also taken for arthritis. There are two parts to the Aloe ferox plant that are used medicinally. The veins beneath the surface of its leaf contain a brown sticky resin that has the beneficial but very bitter-tasting Aloin. And the centre fleshy part of the leaf, clear and non-bitter, that is used in cosmetics and some aloe drinks and reportedly also has wound-healing properties.

The Aloe ferox stands proud, like a warrior, on rocky hill slopes and in both open and bushy areas, from the Cape to KwaZulu Natal. Reaching up to three metres in height, its flowers form a large candelabra-like flower-head around a single stem. Unkulunkulu made them the colour of the sun so that they would stand out and bring warmth to the landscape. He put their medicine in a circle of fleshy leaves so that their leaves could be plucked without needing to remove the plant from the earth. Subtracted from their source in order to make a person whole.

continued on page 72 :: 73

Haworthia species

Haworthia is named after Adrian H Haworth, 1768 - 1833, English botanist and writer on succulents
Used in traditional medicine to treat stomach complaints
Commonly confused with dwarf aloe species like Aloe bowiea

Protea cynaroides

Cynaroides alludes to the similarity of the globe artichoke flower head, *Cynara scolymus*
The name of this species has been unaltered for over 250 years
In 1976 it was announced as the national flower of South Africa

Aloe dichotoma

Common name is Quiver Tree or Kokerboom
The San people used the hollowed out stems for their quivers
It occurs in the Namaqualand and Bushmanland areas of South Africa

Tulbaghia natalensis

Common name is Sweet Wild Garlic
Used as a culinary herb
Cultivated to keep snakes away

Aloe tenuior

Tenuior means very thin
Common name is Fence Aloe
Used in traditional medicine to treat tapeworm
Grows on forest margins

Euphorbia grandicornis

Common name is Rhino Thorn
Grandicornis meaning large thorns
Grows in hot dry areas from KwaZulu Natal through to Kenya
Fruit and flowers are eaten by Vervet monkeys
Thorns raise a painful bump on the skin

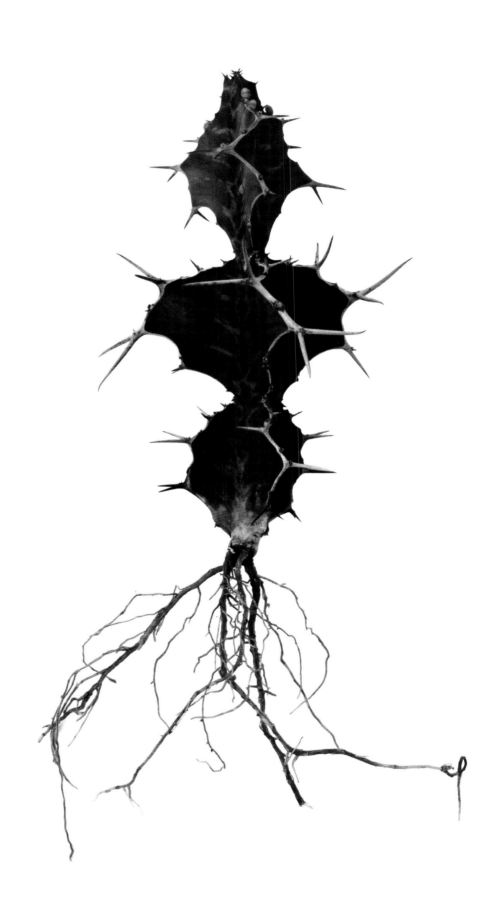

Ficus abutilifolia

Zulu name is iNkokhokho
Afrikaans name is Grootblaarrotsvy
The fruit is edible, yet are nearly always infested with insects

Aloe pluridens

Common name is French Aloe or Fransaalwyn
Pluridens refers to the many marginal teeth of the leaves
This species is not threatened
It is usually associated with impenetrable thicket vegetation

Aloe species

Dwarf aloe +- 100mm tall
Flowers from August to October
Grows in small clusters, rarely as an individual specimen

Aloe pruinosa

Flowers from February to March
Restricted to the Pietermaritzburg district in central KwaZulu Natal
Grows in the shade of trees and shrubs
Conservation status is rare
Zulu name is Icena Elikulu
Afrikaans common name is Slangkop

Unkulunkulu gave man everything that he
needed. He provided more than enough for
everyone. As any man in touch with the land
knows. Unkulunkulu knew that man would
occasionally lose his way and become sick,
so Unkulunkulu gave him the magical gift of
medicinal plants like the aloe. In abundance.
But every now and then, Unkulunkulu grows
weary of man's ignorance and greed. And this
is when the sky darkens so that even the
mighty colour of the Aloe ferox is dimmed.
And the great Unkulunkulu thunders.

Aloe parvibracteata

Flowers from June to July
Grows on rocky outcrops in grassland and amongst trees and bushes
Its centre of distribution is KwaZulu Natal
It also occurs in Mozambique and Swaziland

Aloe microstigma

Flowers from May to July
This species is exceptionally common and is not threatened
Found in a variety of habitats
Microstigma means very small spot

Leonotis leonurus

Common name is Wild Dagga
Used in traditional medicine to treat feverish headaches, coughs, asthma and as a remedy for snake bite
Used as a charm to keep snakes away
Flowers attract a variety of birds, insects and butterflies

Aloe variegata

Sometimes confused with species from the Gasteria genus
A very distinctive Aloe unlikely to be confused with any other species
This species is not threatened
Afrikaans common name is Kanniedood, suggesting eternal life
These plants can withstand extreme conditions of drought

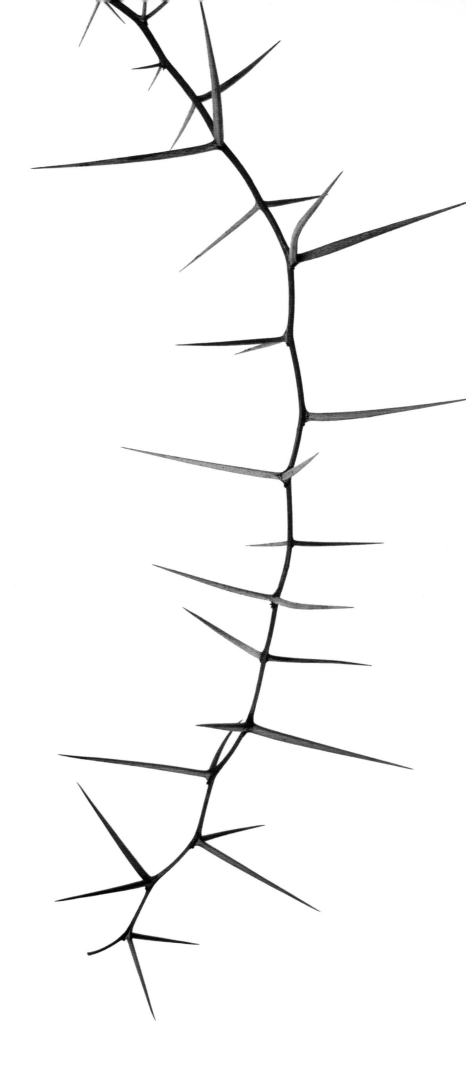

Acacia xanthophloea

Common name is Fever Tree
Medium to large tree occurring in bushveld
Grows on river banks and low-lying swampy areas
Wood provides a general purpose timber
Bark is smooth, greenish yellow and powdery

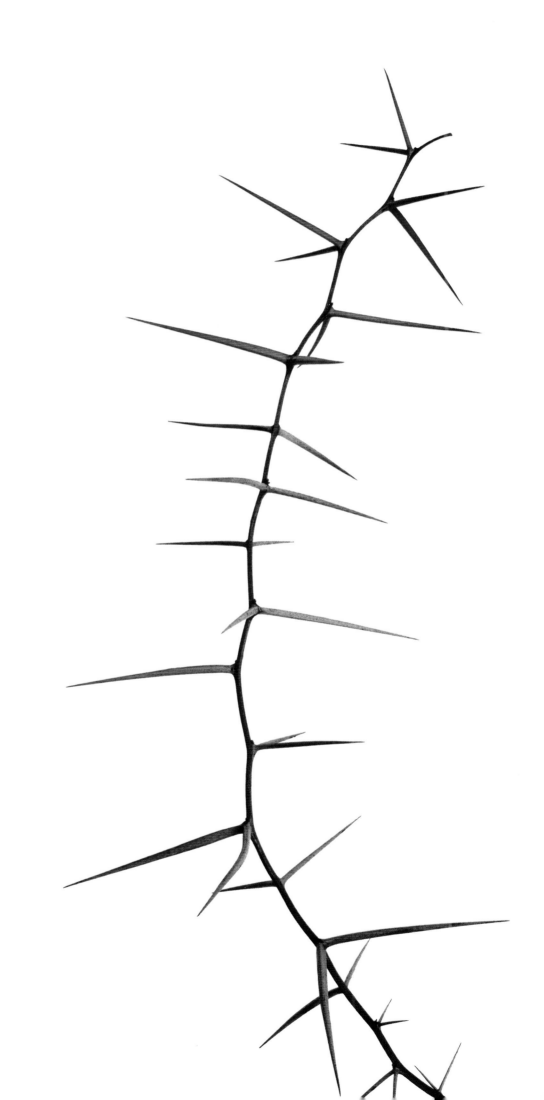

Aloe cooperi

First discovered by the famous explorer Burchell
Rediscovered by Thomas Cooper, after whom it was named
Flowers from December to March
Young inflorescence can be eaten as a vegetable
Used in traditional medicine for easy birth

Lithops bromfieldii

Common name is Flowering Stone
There are about 20 species of Lithops in South Africa
Bushmanland has the highest concentration of Lithops
Very difficult to detect when not in flower, as they look like stones

Gasteria species

Flowers from June to September
Grows in the shade of surrounding vegetation
Used in traditional medicine to treat hysteria and for protective charms

Strelitzia nicolai

Flowers throughout the year
Zulu name is isiGude
Strelitzia is named after Charlotte of Mecklenberg-Strelitz, wife of George III of England
Nicolai Is named after Emperor Nicholas of Russia

Aloe pratensis

Flowers from June to October
Grows on exposed rocky slopes in the high lands of Natal and Lesotho
This species is threatened due to over collection
Sesuto common name is Lekhala Qhalane (the Aloe which opens out)

Bibliography

Wild Flowers KwaZulu Natal, Elsa Pooley, published in 1998

South African Aloes, Barbara Jeppe, published in1969

People's Plants, Ben-Erik van Wyk & Nigel Gericke, published in 2000

The Proteas of Southern Africa, John P. Rourke, published in 1980

Field Guide to Trees of Southern Africa, Braam van Wyk and Piet van Wyk, published in 1997

Guide to the Aloes of South Africa, Ben - Erik van Wyk, published 1996

Acknowledgment & Thanks

Bronwyn Friedman *(wife)* - for putting up with me day in and day out, life is beautiful with you; **Ethan and Ella Friedman** *(kids)* - you are my endless motivation; **Mom and Dad** - for always believing in me and for your amazing support; **Bryan and Liz van Rooyen** *(mom and dad in laws)* - for your lovely daughter and your never ending support; **Sam Arthur Cowan** *(grandfather)* - for my initial introduction to plants, you are my foundation; **Arthur Cowan** *(uncle)* - for introducing me to horticultural; **Jonny Rowe** - for your initial ignition on this project; **Siobhan Gunning** - for understanding this project and hence creating words of wonder; **Trevyn McGowan** - you made this possible; **Anthropologie** - you made this happen; **George Thorne** - for your bounce and encouragement; **Barrows** - for all your education; **Paul Kraus** *(ITI)*- for all your amazing support; **To all who own a piece of my work** - thank you; **Mother nature** - for your endless inspiration.

$\mathcal{P}$hotographer, designer, artist, gatherer of culture, admirer of tradition, maverick, gentle observer, patron of rituals, peaceful philosopher, worldly, African, individualistic, family man. Clinton Friedman is the consummate human whose connection to nature runs deep. Rooted in the beauty of the daily African paradise, Clinton honours his environment and heritage by capturing his uniquely personal perceptions on film. The result is intoxicating to anyone privileged to enter Clinton's world.

Clinton is the owner and image maker behind Fotografik Communications. He prides himself on being dynamic, unconventional and visionary. That is clearly evident in all that he does. Clinton's work is always subtle, sincere and touching. Whatever he does, he thinks about it, feels it passionately, then does it beautifully.

The images Clinton makes may be photographic or pure vector design. Commercial or fine art. Whichever the case, they will show you something in a way you don't normally see or expect it. This is evident in his conceptual, advertising and editorial work, which ranges from studio to location productions.

Clinton not only works on local projects in South Africa, but has also had the opportunity to work in Miami Florida, Atlanta, New York City, London, India, China, Dubai, Mozambique and Singapore.

www.fotografik.co.za

Fotografik Communications
6 Msinsi Road
Kloof
3610
KwaZulu Natal
South Africa

studio@fotografik.co.za

Life is beautiful